UNSUNG

✦

UNSUNG

✦

Emma Purshouse

OFFA'S PRESS
2025

First published in 2025 by Offa's Press,
Ferndale, Pant, Oswestry, Shropshire, SY10 9QD.

ISBN: 978-1-7393618-6-0

Typeset in Baskerville Old Face

Designed by Alex Vann,
printed and bound by Lion FPG Limited,
Enterprise Drive, Four Ashes, Wolverhampton, WV10 7DF

CONTENTS

CONTENTS CONTINUED

Forgotten Tragical, Comical Histories from the Black Country and Beyond

Anne Hathaway finds sonnets written for another woman under the second-best bed and confronts William and his floozy on daytime television!

Sits there; the lyings't knave in Christendom.
So vile a lout! Sir Knob! Bedswerver! Turd!
Man, what a piece of work. Crookback-whoreson!
Three-inch fool, you're not worth another word.

And this woman – an easy glove! My Lord!
She goes off and on at pleasure. Old dog!
Goes to bed to work! Baggage! Base wretch! Bawd!
Hollow-bosoms whore! Stretch-mouth, rooting hog!
I'd throw myself away were I like she.
What a slug. Blue-eyed hag! Leperous witch!
Foul slut. Ye, fat guts, stand farther from me.
Pox on you! You tread on my patience, bitch!

Where we are there's daggers; I'll have her head,
Then help him to his grave; the ape is dead.

A lion speaks to the press

I don't know what had gone on
some argument or other, a grassing up
none of my business, boring people stuff.
Any road up, they shoves this bloke in with me.
Daniel? Yeah…might have been. Anyway
praying all night he was. Pray, pray, pray.
No not prey. Pray. As in prayer. Muttering
on and on to his god. I'd already eaten
so, you know, wasn't interested in him.
They feeds me well here. Lamb, goat, beef,
whole haunches of venison. Then blow me
next morning he claims… You getting this down?
Word for word, mind! … as how angels – yeah, angels –
stopped up my mouth. I'd like to see one try.
Last angel as come in here didn't come again.
Oh no, sir. Spitting feathers for weeks, I was.
Spitting feathers for weeks.

Sir Peter Paul Rubens (1577-1640) was a Flemish Baroque painter. He painted the biblical scene 'Daniel in the Lion's Den' around 1614-1618. The lion lying on the floor to the right of the painting is the lion speaking in this poem.

John Wesley's 'Oss Block Gives Us the Lowdown

A proper short–arse he was. Me, I was his amplification
raising both status and voice up above the crowds.
My support was solid. Unwavering, I was.

And best placed to see that combination of bodily movement,
hand-eye-voice, hear symphony of speech masterclasses
note the big intakes of breath at his perfectly placed

caesura. And, best placed to see the care he took not to sink
his voice too low at the conclusion of a period, to pronounce
last words loud and distinct. And how, when he spoke of love,

he became so soft and smooth. How his joy was full and flowing,
his grief a dull languishing tone, and how when he talked of God
a stronger solemn accent was employed. Solid, I was. Unwavering.

And when the rabble came, some with raised fists at the stopping
of cock fights, some in the pay of the church, some fearful
of being made to sing psalms all day, rise again at five to pray,

we soothed them. And if, sometimes, I felt the slight quake
of knee, a tension at the ankle as a stone flew past his bonce,
I never spoke of it. My support was solid. Unwavering, I was.

And now I stand before you a brand plucked from the burning,
an 'oss block hauled from before the bulldozers, an escapee
of the wages of sin, support still solid, still unwavering.

Full in the knowledge that he would have been a lesser man
without me, and I nowhere now in this world without him.

*John Wesley (1703-1791) was an English cleric, theologian, and evangelist who
was one of the leaders of the revival movement within the Church of England known
as Methodism. The top of the horse block where John Wesley stood to preach in
Wednesbury is preserved in Spring Head Methodist Chapel along with some of the
missiles that were thrown at him!*

Giles

was a sofa surfer
would turn up with his deer
and stop for months.

Sometimes years.
Patron saint of spur makers.
Oh the irony.

He was patron saint
of lying there
suckling at the teat
of other folks'
kindness.

Oh Lord.
you'd hear him sigh
as though doing
nothing… nothing at all
save hiding away
from the world
was all too much.

We never expected
him to get shot.
Accidentally shot.
By an arrow.
A fucking arrow!

Which made him lame.
By which we mean

lamer.

*In its current incarnation St Giles Church in Willenhall dates from 1857.
This poem was written having read about St Giles' 'achievements' on the
wall of the local primary school.*

Victoria Returns to Public Engagements –
Wolverhampton, November 30th 1866

They say you chose our town, our *large and dirty town*
for a kindness that our widows showed you in a letter.

And when you came with *sinking heart & trembling knees*
we did you proud, dressed our streets with ironmongery

and flowers, built you archways from iron bars and coal,
rich pickings wrought from our *infernal regions*.

In cold winds you stayed firm, and curtseyed deep.
Held yourself together. Bore up as coverings *fell well*

revealed your husband's likeness - *Albert the Good,
His Works Follow Him* – seated up on a high horse.

We furnished you with bands, bouquets, scrubbed-up children,
prayers both *long & trying*, then drove you to our station

past *many very Irish looking people, folk in tatters*
who gave *not one unkind look or dissatisfied expression*.

We hear, poor widowed queen, you got home safely,
were *gratified*. Reached Windsor, via Banbury, by 7.

Italicised words in the poem were mined from Queen Victoria's diary entry for the day in question. The diaries are available to read online and searchable using place names.

Matchgirls at Whitsun, 1888

They clatter out of the Paragon
fringed, feathered, foul-mouthed,
singing at voice tops, filling the air
with sparking exuberance. Arm in arm,
a battalion in beer, cheeking the chaps
that cat call from curb sides offering to *treat* them.
Mary doubles up with laughter so hard
she says it makes her teeth ache.
At each alley way and street corner
they turn another girl loose until
only two are left to say goodnight.
Maggie becomes a song disappearing
into darkness. Sarah at the lodging door
hopes Mrs Meany has glued herself to sleep
amongst finished boxes stacked high
on the table. Hopes she isn't waiting up
with a *What time do you call this?*
a *You'll catch it when they lock you out
for half the day,* a whispered *Baggage,*
phossy jaw set to chew so hard at Sarah
she has to look away. Hopes there'll be no
Out on your ear if you don't make the rent,
to follow her up the wooden hill,
to a damp bed shared with a killed mood,
to work rosary beads through her fingers,
pray for change, wake in the night with a start
to see her work things glowing away
on the chair. Like an omen or a visitation.

*The outcome of the Matchgirls Strike in East London in the autumn of 1888
and the Great Dock Strike a year later are credited with leading to the formation
and growth of the labour movement and ultimately the Labour Party.*

*Phossy jaw – phosphorus necrosis of the jaw due to exposure to white phosphorus
used in matchmaking.*

Catherine Eddowes' tin box as a key witness

Please, don't ask me, sir.
I wasn't the only tin box, sir.
The mustard tin she carried her pawn tickets in.
Please, sir, don't ask me to say what I saw,

I wasn't the only tin box there, sir.
There was one of tea, another of matches.
Please, sir, don't ask me to say what I saw.
Ask the two small bags of bed ticking, they'll tell you, sir.

Yes, one of tea, another of matches.
Yes, a mustard tin, and me she kept her sugar in.
Ask the two small bags of bed ticking they'll tell you, sir,
or the needles in the red flannel, they saw it too.

Yes, a mustard tin. And me she kept her sugar in.
So many witnesses, sir. Saw it all with their own eyes,
the needles in the red flannel, sir. Yes, they saw it too, sir.
Ask the clay pipes, and the small tooth comb.

So many witnesses, sir. Saw it all with our own eyes.
Ask the metal teaspoon, and the white-handled knife.
Yes, two clay pipes, and a small tooth comb.
Ask the ball of hemp, the six pieces of soap.

Yes, a metal teaspoon, and a white-handled knife.
Ask the 12 menstrual rags, the thimble, the button.
Yes, a ball of hemp, and six pieces of soap, sir.
Or the red mitten, and the broken spectacles, ask them, sir.

12 pieces of menstrual rag, yes. Thimble and button,
they were there, sir, with the coarse white linen.
Yes, a red mitten, and broken spectacles. Ask them.
Or the three-cornered blue and white shirting,

yes, they were there, sir, with the coarse white linen
and the old apron. The old apron with a repair, sir.
There with the three-cornered blue and white shirting.
And the cigarette case, made of red leather.

Yes, an old apron. Old apron with a repair, sir.
Ask the handbill, and Frank Carter's card.
Yes, a cigarette case. Of red leather, sir.
We were all of us there, sir.

Yes, a handbill, and Frank Carter's card.
Please don't ask me, sir. Ask one of them.
Yes, they were all of them there, sir.
Dumbstruck I am. No words to say what I saw.

*Catherine Eddowes was born in Graiseley Green, Wolverhampton in 1842.
She reputedly stole a tin box from her work place and got the sack, which
meant that she went looking for work elsewhere. Catherine eventually ended
up in London where she died in Mitre Square, Whitechapel in 1888.*

George Boden Cashes in on Little Nell at Tong

What the Dickens are you on about? Not a real grave!
When there it is as large as life – or death, the very spot
where this old church received her in its quiet shade.
Poor Nell. *Polka-dot hanky flourished, sob stifled.*
Past all help or need of it. *Eyes dabbed, nose blown.*
A curiosity indeed but folks are keen to pay their respects.
A fiction, sir? Please check the parish records!
George gestures to the vestry. Ink-stained cuff revealed then quickly hid.
The inclusion of the child's name says fact! Bereft we were
when she passed. The grandfather inconsolable.
Here's his likeness on a postcard, see how sad he looks.
Snivel. Shake of head. This is her, delicately rendered
on a teapot which, for a small cost, could be yours.
Wares to suit all size of purse. Behold the cheaper stuff.
A china plate, perhaps? A bowl? A transfer-printed cup?

*George Boden was the verger at St Bartholomew's Church in Tong, a village
not far from Wolverhampton. He created a grave for Charles Dickens'
fictional character Little Nell around 1910 and then went further in his
attempts to cash in on the tourist trade. Little Nell was the central character
of 'The Old Curiosity Shop' and her journey in the novel took her through the
Black Country. The region is vividly described by Dickens in his work.*

That day

(In memoriam the 19 girls and young women who died in Dudley Port, 6th March, 1922)

6.00am give or take

Maybe she got up, still frowsy with sleep,
babby sister stirring as she creeps out
of the bed they share. Bare feet padding down
the stairs. Huffing out freezing plumes of air,
appearing in the kitchen where Mom pokes at
lazy coal. The coal her step-brothers picked
yesterday off the bonk. And maybe Dad
is sitting in shame or a wing-backed chair
up early as if there was still a job
to go to. And maybe he did say, *Oh, bab...
doh goo today. S'no job for a wench.*
Perhaps Edith smiled, said she could earn
enough to pay the rent. I'd like to think
he put a hand to the child's head as she
bent to lace her hobnail boots. And I'd like
to think she looked back and smiled at him
before she headed off up Factory Road
into the cold smog of a March morning.

Between 7 and 8

I think she whistled as she walked. Waved
to Mr Davies standing on the front step
of the Fountain. I like to think that Mr Davies
(a Woodbine hanging from his lip) waved back.
Maybe our Edith called for Edith Drew
or Nellie Kay, giggling all the way
from Tipton up to Dudley Port.
Cheeking lads who crossed their paths.
Yes, I'd like to think they laughed.

8 am on the dot
The workshop was freezing I should imagine
even with a small stove burning. I expect
they blew on their hands from time to time
as they pushed cartridges through holes
in metal boxes, where with a deft twist
of their agile fingers the young wenches
wrenched free the paper-thin copper
(which might have been the self same colour
as Lizzie Griffiths' hair). I'll bet they bantered
as they separated metals from live ammo
and gunpowder peppered the floor, their clothes.
And I'll bet they rolled their eyes when
Gladys Bryant's mom came to complain
about low wages! *Who's 'er think her is, eh?*
Putting a flea in the ear of management.
Maybe they sang or song or two. Passing hours.

11.45 or thereabouts
I'll bet bellies had been grumbling for a while
not so far off dinnertime. Perhaps Edith heard
the fizz that one girl had reported. I hope she did
and then I hope she heard no more. Not the bang
that blew the roof to kingdom come and sent
the windows flying out. Or that unholy shrieking
as girls ran out to burn in an open yard.

Imagine
youUare
UslateU

that once you lived in the groundUUUUU
Imagine how it was to be thereUUUUUUU
in the cathedrals of mineworkingsUUUUUU
how it was to be split and split and splitUUUU
brushed over with calloused handsUUUUUUUU
How it was to travel from FfestiniogUUUUUUUU
where you were well-versed, schooledUUUUUUUU
in damp. Imagine how it was to be laidUUUUUUUU
on Black Country rooves to the battenUUUUUUUUU
Imagine how much you admired the skyUUUUUUUUU
on those days when the smog clearedUUUUUUUUUU
How you sat in the shadowUUUUUUUUUUUUUUUUUU
of tall chimneys, how moss creptUUUUUUUUUUUUUU
over you. How you took the rainUUUUUUUUUUUUUUU
Held up the snow. Let it all slideUUUUUUUUUUUUUUU
off you again and again and againUUUUUUUUUUUUUUU

What I the Cockatoo in Dudley Zoo
Can and Cannot Do

Cannot
>   fly
>> stand the crowds
>>> understand the curl of their tongues

Cannot
>   stomach the seed
>> undo my tethers
>>> stop plucking at my feathers

Can
>   pose
>> pretend
>>> remember montane and mangrove

>>> the yellow feathers on the
>>>> underside of his wings

*A poem in the voice of the cockatoo pictured in Percy Shakespeare's
painting 'Bird House'. Percy Shakespeare was born in Kates Hill, Dudley
in 1906 and died in Brighton in 1943. He studied at the Dudley Art School
and the Birmingham School of Art. The cockatoo's achievements are unrecorded.*

Goddess of the aspirational working class

Not having a religion but sometimes feeling in need of one
I've made a shrine in the hall to the blue/green lady I bought

at a car boot. On the table below I leave votive offerings,
an orange candle that matches her lips, plastic greenery,

a three-eyed road lamp fished from a skip, occasional post
and reading materials. Today, a book of Dürer's etchings,

and a memoir entitled *Without Warning & Only Sometimes.*
I remember her from childhood of course – Our Lady of the Wall

Over the Neighbours' Gas Fire. Her look of fury
the not-suffering-fools-gladly face. When I pray to her

she doesn't listen much, rolls her eyes. Shrugs even.
And I'm glad. Don't want stigmata, calm expressions. I want her

as she is. A woman you might glimpse in the passenger seat
of a yellow sports car, or scowling from the window of a bus.

Monika Singh Lee aka Monika Pon-su-san was painted by artist Vladimir Tretchikoff
in the 1950s and the image became one of the best-selling prints of the 20th Century.
Monika died in 2017 aged 86.

Ye gods un little fishes...

...thas hot. Eases his feet into the bowl
trousers rolled, stripped down to a white singlet
(new un each Christmas off Bilston market),

the ritual tranklements laid out. Towel,
ointments, creams, crepe bandages, clean socks.
Give us this day our daily bind, lead us not

into more ulceration. Water sluiced away,
re-made legs carry him to the cabinet
like his father before him who art in heaven

he takes a nightcap, a grimace and bear it
slug o whiskey, sleeps in the chair, rises early
walks a foundry floor. Forever. And ever.

Amen.

We imagine ourselves as monkeys in a Victorian taxidermy diorama

The day is water coloured
and a terrifying wind is
at large. The tumult unravels
our ears, ruffles our fur.

It's coming on to work time.
In the distance the school bells
are clanging and the clock
on the mantleshelf jangles our nerves.

The air smells of wet dog
this scene tastes of despair
the ground is sponge and snail shells.
My basket is too small, your umbrella

inside out. Our eyes glass.

Written as a response to a piece of taxidermy on display at Haden Hill House, Cradley Heath.

Overheard Outside *The Works*

She presses her nose to the shop window and looks
There's nothing in there for you, darlin'; it's only books.

Far and Away the Best Teacher There

Amongst dubious priests
and the worrying drama teacher
with the plate in his head,
you stood out, Mr Markiewicz

in your hacking jacket,
with your wire-rimmed glasses
cloud of pipe smoke. I remember
you wore a *Solidarność* badge

though I don't remember doing
anything much in your class save listening
or watching you stare through the window.
You told my parents once

I was a loner like yourself.
I sometimes wonder where you are now
since those days of *1984* in 1982.
Since *Toad of Toad Hall.*

Since *Animal Farm.* Since those days
of kind words for my horror show
homework. I've wondered enough
to Google you, draw blanks where I half-

expected a name on the spine
of a book. Poetry perhaps.
If I'd have found you, Mr M,
I'd have thanked you. For permission

to daydream by example.
For a sense of something else beyond
the line of trees, school boundaries.
For the middle distance.

Unsuitable Places – the YTS girl
from the Old Vic Hotel remembers

I hadn't thought of it for years. How the top floor
where they housed students from the polytechnic
was an obstacle course of leaky roof drips and drops

into pans. How the ballroom smelled of floor polish,
how the only things that ever danced there then
were dust motes. Hadn't thought of Pretty Mandy,

or Pretty Punky Mandy, or sweet Paulette's cow eyes
how they glamourised reception which was both booth,
shop window, and exhibit where punters would come

to check in, oggle and goggle at the charming
of switchboard snakes, deft handling of the SWEDA machine,
smoothing of pencil skirts, to make eye contact

in the slow palming of a key, ask about room service.
Hadn't thought of the duty managers, the blonde one
with the shadowy girlfriend, the dark one with wandering hands

that were once tamed with the sharp edge of a ruler.
Hadn't thought of the yellowing chef with the fag hanging
at the corner of his mouth. The dropped rashers

slipped back into the pan, or the big black women
shuffling wordlessly under the weight of wrapped linen.
Hadn't thought about the mysterious night shifts

of live sex shows, coppers letting their hair down,
or the drinking in of squalid tales over shift-change cuppas,
of being grossed out and not grossed out, shocked

and yet not shocked. Hadn't thought of it at all
'til today. Where is the humanity? the headline runs
200 asylum seekers 'dumped' in city centre hotel.

Kids' faces pixellate in cracked frames. Hung out to dry
washing is bunting in first-floor windows. A red jumper reaches
out its arms. Floral trousers press themselves to the glass.

SWEDA – brand name of cash registers and billing machines

Valeting – circa 1989

Doris works with lint-free rags
stuffed in her overall pouch.
Overflowing. Lighter, fags,
nestling somewhere in there
never too far from her reach.

Autoglym blue fuh windas,
un gold fuh bodywerk.
She's the Mr Miyagi
to my car yard *Karate Kid.*
Polish on, polish off.

She *learns* me about spoodles,
full valets, pitch cars, and sheds,
about how dog hair is a bastard,
how acid bites back and stings
as it flicks up from wheel trims,

how silicone spray for the dash,
and industrial heaters, can,
after one too many winters,
bring on a hard-faced cough
that rattles like the bay door.

She learns me to tut and cuss
when *bleedin' John* on the wash,
who stinks of paraffin,
doesn't get all the *bleedin'* wax off
with the steamer. *The bleeder him.*

Last Tuesday we had eight quid
from down the seats of a BMW
that was meant for the pitch.
Perk of the job she'd said.
Today, a Chubby Brown cassette

out of a glove box. She cackles
all through our dinner break
in the back room up at hers
when we slip the tape into their kid's
ghetto blaster and play it.

Walking back down Raby Street
for the afternoon shift
I tell her I'm jackin' it. She nods.
December it is, and our minds
are as numb as our fingers.

Mr Miyagi was a mentor figure in the 1984 film 'The Karate Kid'.

A man on the 19.34 to Birmingham New Street, having misread the signals, uses his mobile to try to arrange another date with the woman who has hastily waved him off at Liverpool Lime Street

Whah? Say again.
I bet yum freezing
ya baps off ay ya,
bab? Say again.
Say again. Whah?
I could come back
like, warm you up.
Whah? Say again.
Say again. Whah?
Errrrr......Runcorn.
Say again? Whah?
Thursday. Thurs...
Say again. I know,
yeah. Say............
Ok..............Tarrah.
Tarrahtarrahtarrah.

An ode to the short-term memory of the wood pigeon

The wood pigeon
baffled and bruised
sits on a stone
and looks confused.

Ghost shadow dust
on the window pane.
Flown into the glass
again.

I'm in the charity shop

and the man in the orange robe,
whose legs must be cold
is humming a song,

and the woman behind the counter
hums along, begins to sing,
The weather outside is frightful.

Which it is. And then she says,
We've corn to pop!
That's one of the lines. She smiles.

I'm not sure she's right
but I don't tell her so.
And then the man, who might be a Buddhist,

says he prefers *In the Bleak Midwinter*
and so the woman sings that song,
getting the words all wrong.

He joins in, as I thumb through DVDs
not really looking at titles.
When they stop I tell them,

That's a poem by Christina Rossetti that is.
And the woman asks,
Has it got you in the spirit though?

The Christmas Spirit? And I say,
I wouldn't go that far, I mean, it is only October.
The woman behind the counter and the man

who may be a Buddhist laugh and I laugh.
Carry their conversation with me.
Back to the empty flat.

Nets at Number 58

we want to tell you about the cold and the
damp ✳ and the noise of engines ✳ how mufflers on
motorbikes ✳ are no more ✳ we want to tell ✳ how car
tyres sound on tarmac ✳ of the buzz fuzz ✳ background
noise ✳ of the ✳ hum ✳ we want to tell ✳ of the tiny
window ✳ high up in the wall ✳ of the Chinese
opposite ✳ and how it's the exact ✳ size of a human
face ✳ we want to tell ✳ about the ✳ sound of grey and
white ✳ about the warp in the council ✳ car park sign
about ✳ damp slates and whip ✳ of telephone wires ✳
we want to tell how we hide ✳ behind ourselves ✳ and
thick privet ✳ watching ✳ and how it has been like
this ✳ for so long ✳ we want to tell ✳ about the change of
gear ✳ in the car that just passed ✳ the emptying of the
bins ✳ slight variances in the note ✳ of the road as
vehicles run ✳ over ironmongery and ✳ we want to tell
of a birdless sky ✳ and the squinting rain ✳ and the red
brick chimneys ✳ the car horns ✳ and the passing of
things ✳ the endless passing of things ✳ and the dull
ache ✳ for sea that we're too tired ✳ to yearn for ✳ we
want to tell of ✳ emptiness ✳ the sudden slam of a door

Black Country Doldrums, July 2021

After William Matthews

30°. A hiss of air brakes from a council truck.
– Garden Waste Collection Still Only £35 A Year –
Gorra gerrin the shade. A can cracks. *Too warm.*
An' this mask doh help. A lighter clicks.
The bloke eases himself onto a shaded bench.
An oversized dragonfly motif in monochrome
dives down the back of a woman's top.
A yellowing man passes under cracked signage –
Square Deal Carpets and Bedding. Golden Girl
is becoming blue, as some chap kneeling at an altar
of stepladders tears off strips of masking tape.
Shall you still wear yours? A wench tied in the middle
with a red cardie skips alongside her mother
a sideshow freak in a beard mask. On the step
of The Screaming Reaper a tattooed woman smokes.
The queue for the 8pm chemist snakes down the street.
A man on crutches throws back his head to laugh.
I'll wear mine. A pause. *There's people dyin still,*
burrit ay bin said. Two kids skip out the Chinese
become a slap of summer shoes on the square,
the *poc poc poc* of a tennis ball bounced. Tossed so high
it becomes a second sun. Now a small planet falling. 31°

William Matthews (1942-1987) was an American poet and essayist.
His poem 'Morningside Heights' sits between two words 'Haze' and 'Hail'
and was the inspiration for this poem, and other poems in this collection
including the market sequences.

The best concert I ever went to

she was singing just for me. She really was.
Singing just for me. Her moccasined feet
tap tapping and the fretwork on her parlour guitar
intricate, fine. And her voice so strong it filled the air

between us – that beautiful velvet air
she couldn't get enough of. And her face was her face
and yet it wasn't. Transported and transfigured.
Holy. And I saw the slave past of both our houses
and I saw the joy and the love and I saw the God
who she says she prays to.

Redemption Song was low and hard and creaking ships.
And *Universal Soldier* was all the war that ever was
and every damn thing wrong with this world. Religious.
Almost. She segued. *Give Peace a Chance* working in dreamtime
till the light faded and her face changed again,
and she was spent.

Show over.

No, I never saw the oxygen machine, cannula, tubes.

I just saw her song. And the love and hope.

Yeah, that's what I saw. Love and hope rolling on out of her
just rolling on out of her. Yeah. Love and hope rolling on,
rolling on out of her.

Love.

Hope.

On the Waterfront, Merry Hill –
9th September 2022

the statue has her tits out for the lads
that sup at Garrison's Saloon Bar
in their footie tops and baseball caps.

A vaping man jangles car keys, checks
his bumper. A magpie rattles away
to itself in a tree. The ho-hum

of air conditioning. Mind-numbed
pigeons sit on a roof top unaware
a queen is dead. Indifferent to kings.

And what would you have me sing?

A *negro spiritual* says the woman
and for a second her eyes fill with tears
Have I said a wrong word? Is it a wrong word?
And Uche without missing a beat or worrying
about wrong words, begins to sing and instantly
the woman is calm and gazing, cradled in song
cleansed in the Jordan and promise of chariots.

The spell is broken by the rumble of a dinner trolley.
Uche goes to tend to other patients and the woman
wild-eyed asks if the hospital is on fire, if she is
safe here. *Am I safe here? Yes, you are safe here.*
The hospital is not on fire. Hospitals don't catch fire.

Gaza flickers up on the ward TV. We fix our smiles,
grit our lying teeth. Pray a silent prayer for peace.

Lost Girls

Let's not think about
the one that didn't overcome
the counting, the counting, the counting
in multiples of three. Let's not think of her
still there tip-tapping away at light switches
door handles.

Or the one who never had the baby
with the lad who promised her the earth.
said he'd die for her. Then did.

Let's not think about the other who
drank herself half to death.

And let's not go digging up the misfit
still buried in that mining village

or go calling anytime soon
on the one who couldn't cope
with paperwork, went word blind.

And god alone knows we won't be revisiting the one
who settled to a traveller's life, like a duck to dirty water,
only to lose it all. Let's not imagine her wandering
towpaths still. Peeping in at boat windows
cracked like the willow.

Let's leave well alone the one who leans
on the windowsill of a first-floor flat, nose pressed
to the glass. Unable to challenge the neighbours
who dig up her garden. Christ on a bike.

Losers. The lot of me.
Let's not think of any of them.
Ever again.
At all.

We've all got our reasons

The boy asks for change. I have none –
well, none that I want to give. He says he wants
summat from in there takes a hand out of a pocket
and waves it towards Greggs. *Come on* I say.
And we go. Stand at the counter like a couple
of mates who just met up might. He opts for
a margherita pizza slice. *I hope you sort yourself out,* I say,
and what I mean by that is, *you have a beautiful face
and you remind me of someone I used to know
who went your way. And I hope...hope so hard,
you don't go his.* But I don't want to explain that.
Thank you, he says. I don't want to explain any of that
because the last thing he needs, this boy, is some old woman
telling him of the past, making it about the present,
even though sometimes, to her, the two seem
interchangeable, and not so far apart.

Lessons in Life from the Crows in the Memorial Park

Grab as many nuts in your beak
as you possibly can

Take pride in catching nuts
on the bounce

Eat nuts with skins on
or skins off

Wait for the nuts to come

The world will offer you nuts

The world is nuts

Learn to live with nuts

Thank Folio for Shakespeare – a crown of sonnets

I

When I was still a whining snail-paced wench
creeping unwillingly to the school gate
afeared of bullies, Physics, Maths, and French
all those tomorrows and their petty pace

Mrs Derricot, pursed lips, no fun, Eng Lit,
slung out these copies of the Scottish play,
which fell to desks, and sighs, a *What's this shit?*
Homework. Read. Acts one and two fuh Monday.

On the bell, bard, blasted heath and witches
are dropped into sports bags and forgotten
with gym kit and half-eaten sandwiches
which, very much like Denmark, will go rotten.

I'm half–arsed, and don't give a flying Puck.
It's Sunday night before I even look.

II

Yes, Sunday night before I even look.
And I cor mek no sense. No head nor tail.
What fresh hell is this? This babbling book
so foreign to my eyes it could be braille.

This Shakespeare is a jackanapes, a joke!
Who needs to study him this day and age?
Last thing I want's some baldy beardy bloke
canting rubbish. I fly into a rage

as adolescents are supposed to do.
I cast the wretched thing into the bin.
Glare over at it for an hour or two.
Till about midnight on a teenage whim

I fish it out and try it in the air.
Then all that was so foul becomes so fair!

III

Yes, all that was so foul becomes so fair.
In muttering and mouthing I'm proved wrong
the fullness of the rhyme leads me to dare
to test full sound and fury on my tongue.

My fires burn and my cauldrons bubble
unsex me here and take my milk for gall.
Oh! Gray Malkin, ditch drab, toil and trouble
what bloody man is that? It's got it all!

There's boneless gums and nipples, gory locks
there's blind worm's stings and hags and giving suck
carousing, and there seems to be some cock.
Still no clue what's going on, of course, but

devil damn me black, bin a cream-faced loon
cuz all this cussing's great, and what a tune.

IV

Yes, all this cussing's great, and what a tune
but back in class I keep my mouth shut tight
I've learned enough of ropes to read a room
you don't want other kids to think you might

find modicums of interest in a book.
Therein lies the way to a swift shoein'.
There's daggers in kids' smiles when you look
such keenness is the road to rack and ruin.

So I kept my head down, held my questions.
Though I gleaned stuff from when the teacher spoke
made sense from her various suggestions
a Coles guide and my scanty study notes.

Result. Amongst my Us and Ds there sat
a big fat fuck off A. Well, fancy that.

V

Yeah. A BIG FAT FUCK OFF A. Fancy that.
It led to YTS schemes and the dole
the in and out of work, the 80s crap
outrageous fortunes, life without a soul.

And dreams, Midsummer Night's or otherwise
were knocked out of us. Pinched, then punched, then squashed.
Our courage screwed and sticking. Thatcherized.
Futures? Nah, mate. Things of the past. They're quashed.

Dead ends and boredom start to sicken me
until the day I had this chance encounter
with the fates. The sign. An epiphany.
In sonnet terms…it might've been a volta.

Deep in Road-to-Damascas bargain basket
there lurked ex-rental video of Hamlet.

VI

And this ex-rental video of Hamlet
reminds me just how much I'd loved the bard
and even though I hadn't really planned it
I turn my thoughts to college. Though it's hard

I take next steps. Enrol myself on classes.
Learn of Chekov, Kafka, and of Ibsen.
And this new found interest in the classics
it's down to Billy S… and Mel Gibson.

Reading like a demon, penning essays.
The years of work and grim determination.
I even take a small part in a play.
My ideas now are well above my station.

Somewhere along the line there came degrees
though academics mattered less to me.

VII

Yeah, academics matter less to me
than power of words lifting from the page
the tumble-twist of rapture as they're freed
to strut and fret their stuff across this stage

disturb the atoms, ring out like a gong
to rend the air with sighs and shrieks and groans
fall trippingly both on and off this tongue
to shake a wall's foundations with a moan

make much ado about…well, everything.
Zounds, this performance poet's gateway drug
was soar and dip of Shakespeare taking wing
that piquant taste of tragedy and love.

Respite from bullies, Physics, Maths and French
when I was still a whining snail-paced wench.

Modern Instances
– Midsummer to Twelfth Night –

Trade and Commerce – hourly intervals of a midsummer market day

4.45am – sunrise

The ends of metal market stores are arrows
pointing to the heavens. A group of people gather,
a ringing phone, a gruff voice more engine than human
counts *6, 5, 8* becomes indistinct again. A pillar box

pouts and above the drinkers a hot red tick is picked out
on the Savers shop front. Health. Home. Beauty.
A satellite dish is an ear. A tree leans in
makes out the words *sister son*. A peachy sky peeps

over the top of the buildings on the far edge of the square
is greeted with sneezing, the remnants of night.

5.45am

Birdsong. A flap of pigeon wings
a man in black – black shirt, black shorts
black socks, black trainers – saunters
past Dr Tonks's clock with its lamp arms
raised either side of its shocked face

above the Barrel and Shive, now
a foot clinic, the sky is bluer than the van
a man in a baseball cap is unpacking
boxes starting to appear on boards
under a blue and white plastic awning

on the main road there is traffic
and a bus engine turns over and over
two pop bottles roll on their backs
above them spiked windowsills, a missing tile
another flap of pigeon wings. Birdsong.

6.45am

A blonde woman in black gloves wears a brown mini-skirt
and a green apron and carries nine crates piled one on top
of another past Square Deal Carpets and Bedding over to the
greengrocer's stall. Her white legs flash as she walks.

A shop alarm stirs the stiff woman on the bench from her
phone scrolling under the depiction of the locksmiths, nubs are
scattered like a wedding of smokers not long happened here.
Groan. Stretch. She mounts her electric scooter like it's a horse
whirrs off along the shadowed side of the street, hi-vis muted
by gritty roll of wheelie bins, one pushed one pulled.

A radio begins to play. Light catches tree tops.

7.45am

Seeds floating, scudding, drifting, lazy in comparison
to purposeful walk by man with rucksack and hi-vis,
woman sporting ponytail, take-out coffee, Nike tick
her energy huge at her back. The Union Jack on The Bell Inn
is the quiet click of its halyard. A blue tarp billows
like a ragged sail on a Marie Celeste market stall where
fierce toilet rolls are caged. A man with a slight limp
walks like a gun slinger. Zorba's Grill is shuttered.
To Let. To Let. Conway's Butchers are still High Class
have owned, since 1929, the only apostrophe in town.
A man with a stick, walking as though he's lost sheep
wanders towards their door. The school uniform stall
is still in shadow. A pigeon is a black finial on a roof
against blue sky. Seeds still floating, scudding, drifting.

8.45am

Market Street is blocked to cars by a blue barrier, chunky
like a giant Duplo brick. A man arranges a dangle of chains.
The Spuddy Marvelous van shutter moves like it might just
be about to open. Clank of cutlery. A box of *Farm Fresh 50's
Baking Potatoes* fidget on the step. Hopeful people peer
into closed charity shops. Empty bags hung over forearms.
A woman tries on a ring, turns her hand this way, then that.
Another in a hot pink top rides her bike, with hot pink forks,
straight in through the open door of Euro Express.
A tiny child scoots by on a no-pedal bike, mumbles Chinese
to an imaginary friend, Pikachu blushing on his rucksack
as a woman picks up two rolls of bin bags, her stripy vest
a match for the trousers of another woman behind. A meaty man,
headband, shades and gloves, stays seated on his meaty bike to
consider a Reggae Magic Honey Puff Mag Jar. *Laa la laa laa* plays
on *Laa la laa laa* the Fruit and Veg stall. *Laa la laa laa. Hey, Jude.*

9.45am

Outside Compton Care, the Mobile Citizens Advice Unit
is parked up. A woman zipped into a black hoody

has purple hair, has fetched drinks for the two men sitting
on the bench. *Yours is fuckin dearer than a can.*

Hands Pepsi Max to the one who says he doesn't drink.
The vape stall trader moves to lean on a green bin. *I'm horny,*

horny, horny, horny sings Pepsi Max man. Sunshine loosens
tongues, *Beautiful day today. Pukka day today. Tuesday's hottest 25.*

*Be looking for cheap sun tan lotion in a bit. Gunna get me
another posing pouch, ay I. Get one of them white hankies,*

you'll look like an Arab. Too much for me down here yesterday.
Too much says the boyman with the hard-luck eyes addressing
his feet

or the floor. Purple-haired woman *ony got out of hospital yesterday.*
Been on a sesh again, ay I. Knocked me abaht. Purple-haired woman

con goo two days without, but then has to have a spliff. *I cor get my*
head down without a spliff. Purple-haired woman has no teeth,
smiles anyway

as a tidy lady with Supremes' hair and drips of pearl and gold
hanging at her ears takes the weight off, waits her turn for advice.

10.45am

By Dr Tonks' clock people queue and wait for bin bags
and boxes to be unloaded from a truck or brought forth
from a shop front. A man with a beard takes three
loads them into his orange bike trailer that might
once have held children, and cycles away. Bits and Bobs
says the signage giving no clues. Posh Nails Has Moved
a poster in the window disassociates, absolves itself.

A masked hooded man on a bike, stops, puts on gloves
like Marcel Marceau might have worn to mime
a robbery. A man with fresh notes leaves the cashpoint.
A woman, so pale she's ice cream, joins the queue
for a box, oxygen cylinder at her back heavier than she is.

Today on two sides of Dr Tonks' clock it's shady.
Petunias and pansies struggle in stone troughs,
ears of wild grasses whispering around them and
the cast-iron lion set up to his nose in concrete.

An ambling man's T Shirt claims NIRVANA as he passes.

11.45am

The woman in the Vauxhall has taken a wrong turn
is trying to spin round and go back the way she's come
facing now the snake of cars that fill the one-way street
their blaring horns drowning out Sidney Walker's butcher's bark
as he leaves the smell of hot pork sandwiches to do his work.

Follow him on Facebook. Blue crates of gammon
stacked up in the doorway declare themselves to be two
for a fiver. A couple weeble over to the window. She has hair
the colour of wireworms, it glows in the sun as they
consider *minted lamb shanks, salmon cut beef joints.*

12.45pm

Clouds scud, seeds have raised themselves up to another
level, a pale-skinned, dark-haired woman lets herself
into a door at the side of Golden Girl where Elvis, in 3D
on purse and bag, is caught between two dimensions,
appearing at a glance as a skull, a memento mori next to
the lime green and fuchsia pink doily tops and no one
seems to notice. Not the man in the bucket hat or the
shaven-headed woman riding the disability scooter, a punk
shock of cockscomb hair sprouting from the front of
her head, not the shoppers with bulging bags, nor the woman
in salwar kameez nor the child with corkscrew curls,
just like his mom's, who waves two windmills coloured
foil turning, refracting light. Not the tantrumming kid
in the Woody suit, so many cowboys on one mustard-
coloured ground. Not the man in combats with an anvil face
who smokes as he rides a woman's bike, nor the youth
TikTokking in the Spuddy Marvelous queue. And certainly
not the couple who walk with unmatched guide dogs. And
not the people in the plane that draws the ear first and then
the eye upwards towards a midsummer sky towards four swifts
skimming the blue yonder. Swifts which go unnoticed like
3D Elvis bags, and the wonders that are *this seasons* doily tops.

1.45pm

The man with black plaits has a girlfriend with long legs
or the woman with long legs has a boyfriend with black plaits
it isn't really clear. A man blue-turbaned stands by holding a yellow
bag while his wife, her hair scraped back into a bun, admires jewellery.

Red Bull is drunk. Between customers stall holders nibble at food
snuck from white paper bags. Bench men discuss energy bills, swig
Tyskie lager. A man with a flop of hair and a comedy tie pockets a
purchase wrapped in blue plastic. The sun is hot now. And nobody
feeds the pigeons as signs request.

2.45pm

A man in a woolly hat rests his arse on an empty stall.
Comedy Tie Guy holds onto a pole like he's standing on a bus.
The vape man's stock is already packed up in boxes.
Talk turns *They try to catch you out* to PIP assessments.

A man in a waistcoat that suggests a Greek wedding
talks to another who has bowed his head to his phone.
A youth on a bike with *sofn'free* hair, rides alongside
friends who walk. A girl in short shorts holds her own space.

Outside Ladbrokes a man peers at his phone
like he needs new glasses, or an overdraft. And England are,
as always, bringing it home in the window. Tens of people
walk away from market place. A dog barks.

A couple meet head on. He's on his way to football
she's showing off her Friday night nails. As the breeze
picks up a little, people go in and out of the Post Office.
Outside Blunts in baskets summer shoes bloom.

3.45pm

The Spuddy Marvelous van glides off a wooden chock,
is coupled to a 4x4, towed away leaving a patch of soapy liquid.
The fruit and veg trucks disappear. The hard-luck-eyed man
helps load the vape van. Children plucked from school chatter.
Under a bonnet an AA man fixes. *Happy Pride Month*
the sticker in the Compton Care window shouts. Litter bowls
along the market place as the fruit and veg woman whizzes home
on a green electric scooter the colour of her conference pears.
The brickwork curves of buildings reappear as the *well nice*
woman from the baker's stops, chats to the vape lads.
A woman on a disability scooter wears a mask slung low
like the jeans of the lads taking selfies. The stalls return to board
and metal arrows pointing at the sky. Drugs are trundled
into the 8pm Chemist on a sack truck as an African woman glances
up Wolverhampton Street, walks like she is water past the smoker
in the Compton Care apron pacing the length of the window.
The lads in low-slung jeans carry off a jumbo pack of toilet roll.

4.45pm

Teenagers appear in groups. A girl with a long dark plait
scoots along on a pink scooter, her mother rests a hand
on a pregnant belly as she rolls along behind. Once upon a time

Irn Bru tasted phenomenal from T/A Greens. A poster
for a fun fair that happened months ago is fading and
windows above Euro Express are whited out in swirls.

A brick has taken out some glass, and a u from s n beds.
Clouds are greying, the sunshine is gone. Fag butts animated
suddenly by the wind skip along the square then settle.

5.45pm

Cries from a toddler are travelling from an upstairs room.
A man on a bench seems deflated like his football. Sneezes.
The toddler cries some more. Then more. Then cries again.
A motorbike jags from an alleyway. Car horns. A jangle of keys.
Vehicles travel up and down the market place drown out the
toddler for a moment. Windows open in flats above shops,
let   out   their   heat.

6.45pm

Hip Hop. Grime. Beats. Tunes. Mixup and mashup.
Cars compete. Sitting on the low step of Euro Express
a man scrolls through his phone, stands, gives a thumbs up
to the world, turns, wanders back in. A boy takes a seat
on a bench between a woman in a protective boot and
a woman in sandals. On the street corner a young couple
stand, touch at every opportunity. A man in a jade turban
and plaid shirt holds his phone with two hands as he walks.
A curtain shifts gently in an upstairs window. A red car
passes. Ubers cruise. A baby points from a pushchair.
A young girl in a judo suit lags behind. The 8pm Chemist
is still open. Two assistants talk at the till. Clock watch.

7.45pm

Cardboard is piled high outside Bits and Bobs.
A seagull takes ownership of the evening air.
A signpost points in wrong directions and towards
a police station that is no longer there. Wind ruffles
feathers and litter. An empty street is entered briefly
by a teen on rollerblades…gliding effortlessly out again.
The Union Jack on The Bell flutters in stops and starts.
A blue neon light reflects in an empty shop window
switches to purple. The teen skates out of Angel Passage
short-circuiting the town. Back again she comes.

8.45pm

Two groups of folk at either end of Market Place.
By Tonks's clock Asian men have come down
from brooding rooms above the shops. To take the air.
And drink. And talk. And one to rub his long bare leg
up and down. Up and down. By the board that welcomes
all to Willenhall the white folk sit. The woman in the boot,
the one in sandals and the boy have now been joined by men
and a dog rolling on its back. They've come to take the air
and drink and talk. The shutters down. A seagull flying.

What else to do but drink
                    and talk and drink
                                    and talk some more.

9.37pm – Sunset

The Victorian lamps are lit
above the Tattooed Reaper
though the arrows of the stalls
point to light left in the sky.

A ball bounces somewhere
round a corner. An African couple
swiftly stride to beat the dark
back home, a pushchair folded,

carried, and baby strapped
and sleeping at the woman's back
a surprise of curls, a peaceful
perfect face. *Hello* they say *Hello*

walking on into twilight under grey sky
that holds a hint of dusky pink
as brickwork starts to glow warm
and orange in this our evening's golden hour.

Town Square Haiku

An ambling man farts
in heat of late afternoon
begonias wilt

A quiet corner

Seen from this council bench, attributed to ADRIAN
who has scratched through green Hammerite
to reveal himself in red oxide undercoat

the fishing pool is a single flag iris
a gusting of wind, the moving reeds
a tricking of light, the animation of

a plastic heron, the scattering of
small balls of black fluff
fearing for their lives

the coming on
of rain.

It's grim here

though nobody's told Roger
nor the whitethroats nor the blackcaps

nor the willow warblers
so here they all are

him with his bins, them singing
from the hawthorns

dawn love songs to the blue brick
metal corrugation and graffiti

In the bread shop

we are bemoaning the stealth privatisation
of the National Health. The old man
(crusty cobs, medium-cut white loaf)
says he went to the eye infirmary
that he was there an hour and seven Indians
went in before him. *Seven Indians!*

The woman behind the counter and I
roll our thankfully working eyes. It's then
I realise that as I haven't spoken out
neither me nor her will know if rolling eyes
are due to *Seven Indians* going in before
or down to an old bloke trotting out his tropes.

At home, I find I have been given brown
not granary. Embrace the change. Make toast.

View from the beer garden – day time

A rude dog barks over traffic and trains.
A swastika is burnt into the grass
on the scrubland beyond the low fence.

An old man white-haired red–shirted
walks bow-legged to a younger man's car.
With a bleep he opens the driver's side door.

Backyard

If you sit here with me for long enough
the train noise and the sound of dropped weights
at the gym will soften into dark. And the gentleness
of pigeons will take themselves off to bed. And the
bees will drift away from the lavender and the ants
will disappear. The crows will shut themselves up
in nests and the speedy cars with their showy exhausts
will fall silent. It is then that the hedgepig will tiptoe
in under the gate on his long legs to meet
with the fox in the moth-filled dark, sip water
from the bowl as the wood mouse moves in blinks
from the shed to our feet. And the wild weeds
crazed in July heat will sing then their mad lullabies
to shadowy plane trees, ivy-clad red brick and dereliction.

'hedgepig' is an alternative name for hedgehog

Baiting Up

Two giggling girls in grey are circling the fishing pool.
Boys lean on brick walls, lollop in grass. Phones ping,
music is distorted by distance and yap yap dogs,

a handful of maggots has been cast onto seed-heavy
green water. Adidas-striped man with red rod
stands as though he may be No.7 on the sculpture trail.

Here, at the quiet end, tight to water lilies a fish back
breaks the surface, rolls like a leviathan might,
sinks again, *Nice 'N' Spicy Nik Naks* packet barely shifting.

In the Memorial Park – Remembrance Day

Two crows dog fight it out over a playing field
as a woman with toggles strides down the path
one hand pocketed, the other swinging like

something mechanical. A man with sculpted hair,
skinny-fit jeans, black sports bag, styles it out
sunlight strobing and cross-hatching his arm.

The flats in distant Wednesfield
have been painted to match the sky.

Counting the Stops on the 529

Next stop a man in high viz walking *Newlands Close.*
Next stop Summer Street with blue sky and new builds
where work has ceased. *Next stop Portobello Island*
and a woman in pyjamas unlocks the door at 23,
pneumatic drills vibrate, a removed alarm has left
a heart shape. The war memorial sports a poppy wreath,
an RAF roundel. The public art on the roundabout is
a lock mechanism. *Next stop Noose Lane.* Seats rattle.
Next stop Cleveland Close. No Parking. Keep Clear.
Council houses without gardens. Red lights. Red brick.
Trees tired and netted. A blue wheelbarrow stands
in a front yard. *Next stop* Sikhs carrying plasterboard
Deans Road. Next stop Hurstbourne Crescent where
a moss-green telegraph pole is a ship's mast, held up
by rigging. *Next stop Mayfield Medical Centre.* Woman
in a red anorak, a second riding a disability scooter.
Next Stop Plascom Road man with B&M Home Store's bag
ferrets for bus fare is welcome to join St Matthew's Church.
Next stop Old Heath Crescent the Baitul Atta Mosque has
love for all and hatred for none. Next Stop Hickman Avenue
the driver is blind to a plodding woman, quilt coat, white hair.
A black crow flaps. *Next stop Corser Street.* Metal flames
flare at the gates of the Park and Ride. *Next stop* coal bags
and gas bottles *Minerva Wharf. Next stop Shakespeare Street*
plywood shears away into beards. *Next stop Ward Street.*
A red light. A yellow grit box. Jennings touts tidy deaths
and a clean car park. *Next Stop Wolverhampton Bus Station.*
A hooded man walks in a subway. A blue tram crosses
a bridge. Ames has left their mark in spray paint.
Trust in Allah says the bold sign on the side of the X8.

Advent

The shutters are down
on the Caribbean place

they've prepped and long gone
though upstairs a TV is on

or maybe it's just reflected light
from the faux-Victorian street lamp.

Somewhere else in town
a boy is opening

a calendar window
discovering snowflakes.

Trade and Commerce – hourly intervals
of a mid-winter market day

8.16am – sunrise

A couple in padded jackets watch shop fronts
for signs of life. At the Pit Stop Mini Market
lights are on. Pringles shine like gifts from
the magi. A man in camo, a black hat pulled low,
stands at the school uniform stall, flask in hand,
pacing slowly. A woman walks a low-lying
hairy dog into a darkened alley. The clinking
of bottles. Ladbrokes is heavy-lidded, snoozes
in a faint red sleepy glow. A man carries
a blue plastic bag. A motor scooter coasts in,
engine cut as though not wanting to wake
the town. The clinking of bottles. The clinking
of bottles. No customers at the fruit and veg stall.
No customers at the vape stall. The clinking
of bottles. Insistent. Now frantic. Now a smash.
Spooked a ginger cat runs his little legs
towards an unopened post office.

9.16am

The vape stall plastic sheeting blows like a sail.
Pigeons peck at sludge. Two women roll along
with side-to-side gaits. Spuddy Marvelous man
unloads a gas canister. A man in black with a flat cap
looks back. Voices are muffled. *You ony got the one?*

A woman's black beehive is a separate entity.
A roll of wrapping paper a chimney on a shopping bag.
Car horns. The metal arrow of a still-empty stall points
to flat grey sky. A road cone lies spark out
next to a telephone box with no door and no windows.

10.16am

Quality is the Future at Sidney Ward's Butchers
Boneless Turkey Crowns from £45.99

Tadaa says a woman leaving. *Never Say Never*
shouts a man. A woman clutching a list passes.

Another with folded arms and blue latex gloves
is a bouncer in charge of hot pork sandwiches.

Under see-thru umbrella a woman with turned calves
is a jar of mustard clip clipping down the pavement.

In a two-child buggy a baby sleeps and a toddler
in a red bobble hat is a parcel in a pile of shopping

an older brother walks, Mom pushes for home
Dad follows laden and tattooed about the head

with a winged beast. Wind gusts and a Walsall Council
bin bag becomes a jellyfish of the air. Sudden. Ethereal.

11.16am

In the yard at The Bell, circa 1659, cardboard shepherds
collide with a crocheted twelve-foot fall of red poppies
Lest We Forget a woman in a leopard-skin coat unbuttoned
over a red velvet dress takes a photo on a phone as tinsel
sways gentle on the railings. The Bell Alley wall blows
two metal kisses to the world and in the leaded window
Victorian carol singers are inanimate behind condensation
and dummy snowflakes. Above, the Union Jack has its own pole
in a headlock. A string of dull lights are stranded seaweed
strung out from one side of the damp square to the other.

12.16pm

Christmas All Wrapped Up at Compton Care.
A man has bright blue shorts that match his plastic bag.
A pigeon cocks its head to one side, and seems surprised,
a Yorkshire terrier far away from home and dressed in hi-vis
sniffs. The hard-luck eyed man shelters under the vape man's
awning a tinny tune playing on the radio on the fruit and veg stall
is indecipherable, a man checks the contents of a brown envelope,
a woman with braided hair carries a card in a paper bag. A van
stops, rolls a window, orders jacket tatas. Blue peppers the sky.

1.16pm

The man from the cheap shop with no name
is already wheeling away his stock from the stall

as an awning flaps and flutters. FOR SALE
offers the sign outside a boarded-up

Gravestock & Owen Chartered Accountants.
Schink. Grainy flip of a Zippo lid. Smell of petrol.

In the window of Crazy Wicks is a dreamcatcher.
A man with a blue-inked face holds the hand

of a little girl in a red coat with tan fur collar
as she totters in chonky boots. Santa is watching

from Conway's window, behind him a side of pork
hangs. A man in a damson turban walks a wife

who ambles at his side. The arrow on the weather vane
on Dr Tonks's clock points away from town.

A man chewing cud comes from The Bell's yard,
a second man follows carrying crisps, a third in shorts

has a bobble hat bedecked with Christmas puds,
a fourth reads a poster for the Nativity Trail.

A woman with a figgy pudding face lights a fag,
a fur trim on a hood becomes mutton-chop whiskers

as a green and white sail awning pulls free
hits the deck, is towed away. A child coughs.

2.16pm

Any three for a fiver now to clear 'em up.

A man with a pink turban talks with his hands.
The red fake flowers, and the plastic trees are not
selling. A woman in a tight red silk hood
has a Bulls' sweatshirt, Mickey Mouse
on the sleeve of her coat, a Grinch on her bag.

A woman with purple hair walks quickly, another
answers a phone, a third dons blue headphones
with a gold star. A man's shoes squelch.
A woman with a white Alice band drags a trolley.
Five people stare through a window at meat.

3.16pm

Near Court 1 bins overflow, and a shopping trolley has crashed
into an egg box. A Polish-speaking family are wandering,
a man kicks a bag that used to contain *fragrant jasmine*
then limps on. A council truck drives towards the clock.
A little girl with two snaking plaits runs in clumpy shoes.
A woman in a face mask carries a Sports Direct bag.
A ladder scales a wall, footed on the canopy above the shops.
The Spuddy Marvelous serving hatch is shut.
A blonde woman in black leans to grab a net of veg.
In Golden Girl's window a woman picks up a fallen bobble hat,
arranges tinsel stoles around the shoulders of Elvis bags.

3.54pm – sunset

A charcoal tree is sketched out
on the peach and blue-grey
ground of the sky. A steely
block of flats appears distant.

The windows above Blunts
are a wall of shoeboxes.
Newspapers past are bagged up
waiting outside Ladbrokes.

On the main road a bus rumbles.
Outside Posh Nails girls gather.
Too cold to hang around
a can of Red Bull rolls away.

The fairy lights are twinkling.
A child cries. A little girl in pink
shouts *Merry Christmas* high and clear
Merry Christmas high and clear.

JESUS IS STILL LORD & SAVIOUR

is the gospel according to the sign over the travellers' church
and inside the singing is puffed-up full-throated. It floats   out
through the tiled porch, through the turquoise arch   out

over the top of the 4x4s with their cattle-bar bumpers out
to Morrisons' car park, to the trolleys in their shelter
and on to the outside garden centre. At the door

of The New Testament Church of God
(Willenhall Tabernacle) a man is frantically flapping
his black umbrella like he's shoo shooing a crow.

Sly dig singing of bigger congregations nip at Sunday
heels as he turns to enter the house of his Father.

Double decker

Next stop Portobello Island. A woman speaks resignedly
into her phone. The phone speaks back in something which
might be Spanish. The woman coughs and sniffs. *Next stop*

Noose Lane. A man in black with shoes the size of small boats
takes a seat and stares mournfully out of the dirty bus window.
A British Gypsum lorry glows cerulean blue in winter sunshine.

Up Town

Alarms sound, pigeons strut, a woman in a hijab strides
past a man who is smoking weed and waving one arm.

Charlie's Fish Bar is closed. Alarms still sounding.
A man wears camo, hides inside a hood. LIFE's window

is a swish of satin, a woman rearranging a wedding
dress. Bird shit adorns GLAZE's glass. Alarms. Still. Sounding.

Today we invite all the creatures
we meet on our walk to dinner

We *cronk* an invitation to the raven that passes overhead
tell it *Sandwiches on the menu. Granary bread from
Swiss Oven. And cheese, extra mature from Lidl,
and oh...the chutney with plump, juicy raisins.* He flies on.
Perhaps he has heard. Perhaps not. It is winter

the newts and frogs are hiding. We ask them anyway
not wanting them to feel left out. The fat squirrel
comes close, takes nuts offered from the tips of our fingers.
Our house...dinnertime...more of this...more of the same.
It looks at us, seems to comprehend. At the top pond

we call to the white rumps of the jays the same invitation.
Nobody is left out, not the three sleek rats who scamper
and scurry away into the tangle of undergrowth.
Not the russet fox who watches us slant-eyed
from the undergrowth. Not the robin who perches

next to us on the bench. *More of these porridge oats*
we promise *when you come to dinner today at ours.*
We tell it to tell the great tit in the hawthorn
who is waiting, just out of earshot, for us to leave
so it might feed. We ask the fish and the heron

the shovellers who are busy spinning in their steady
steady circles, ask the crows in the park. Feel sure that all
will come. At dinnertime we open the windows look
to the sky, to the damp earth, to the plane tree branches
and tops of limes, check the drains, open the back gate

to a distant bark. A raven flies overhead, cronks out
a laugh. We eat our sandwiches, put away the mealy worms
cheese, oats, biscuits. *Tomorrow* we say, *we'll do the same*
because Rome and bridges, worlds and trust are not
rebuilt in a day. Yes, tomorrow we will do the same.

Will ask again.

If 'e sees a squirrel 'e'll goo

'e woh urt ya
ex racer
opens 'e ran
Irish tattoos in 'is ears

Peregrine Billy

if we was walkin' 'im
way back when
we'd be locked up

they was for rich men
and princes
I've read abaht it

'ad 'im since fust lockdown

th'other died
they lay on the bed
together

I like to think 'e towd 'im
yal be olright 'ere

look at 'im

spring soon

we'll tek 'is coat off then

*This poem was written to document a typical Black Country
one-sided conversation, in this instance, about a retired greyhound.*

New Year

As the kings and queens offer up their resolutions
the trumpet of last year resounding and promises of this

ringing in our ears we find at Bumble Hole
the Conservation Group Visitor Centre is, as the sign claims,

OPEN. A bench back on the far bank of the cut
is liquid silver, trees are still, a motorbike distant

as summer. Today Cobbs Engine House is our overseer.
A minute off. A skate of ducks. Slow melt of cat ice.

Epiphany – an A to Z of why this Sunday our patch of scarred scrubland is better than your patch of scarred scrubland

Amen and halleluiah there we have it
bolt of blue lightning, sparking the air
coming to us from the murk of winter over
disused railway tracks and abandonment
easy as you like over our sweet dereliction,
flooded quarry pits, and graffitied badlands.
Glory be to capped mineshafts.
Halcyon days have only gone and returned
in the wide-eyed surprise of this broken
January morning. Igniting the dreary day,
kick-starting the new year, lifting and
lighting the fiery forges of despondent hearts,
Mother Mary, and all the saints. Praise be.
Never in a month of Sundays did we expect this
over here, over our wretched spoil mounds.
Praise be and bowed bulrushes, to this blessing
quickening the being of the Black Pool
raising the dead spirits of us all. Hail to you
saving our souls on this Sabbath day.
There! Look to the wild thing, harbinger of hope,
unasked for but welcome miracle of miracles,
visitation in a mired, mithered winter. There!
Water god passing through our unholy firmament.
X marking its spot on the map of the morning.
Yee hah to this Zip–a–Dee–Bastard–Doo–Da
Zip–a–Dee–Blow–Me–Down–Kingfisher–day!

Acknowledgements

'Anne Hathaway finds sonnets written for another woman under the second-best bed and confronts William and his floozy on daytime television!' was previously published in *Anne-thology: Poems Re–Presenting Anne Shakespeare* (Broken Sleep Books, 2023).

'A lion speaks to the press' previously published in *Prole* magazine.

'John Wesley's 'Oss Block Gives Us the Lowdown' was written as part of a series of promenade performances that took place in Wednesbury in the Black Country. This was a Multistory project.

'Matchgirls at Whitsun, 1888' was runner-up in the 2020 Matchgirls Memorial Poetry Competition and subsequently published in *Feathers And Pennies: Poems and Stories for the Matchgirls.*

'Catherine Eddowes' tin box as a key witness' came 3rd in the National Poetry Competition in 2021, and was published on The Poetry Society website and in *The Poetry Review* spring edition 2022. Later published in *It's Honorary, Bab,* 2022. A video of this poem is available to watch at www.poetrysociety.org.uk/poems/catherine-eddowes-tin-box-as-a-key-witness

'That day' was created as part of a series of promenade performances that took place in Tipton in the Black Country, and was later published in *Tipton Tales,* Multistory. A video of this poem is available to watch at www.youtube.com/watch?v=Y3v7DpSUOAg

'Goddess of the aspirational working class' was commended by the judge, Deb Alma, in the 'Sonnet or Not Poetry Competition' 2024.

'Ye gods un little fishes...' was highly commended by the judge, Adam Horovitz, in the 'Gloucestershire Open Poetry Competition' for 2021.

'Unsuitable Places – the YTS girl from the Old Vic Hotel remembers' was published in *The Bread and Roses Poetry Award Anthology*, 2021.

A version of 'Valeting – circa 1989' was published in *The Bread and Roses Poetry Award Anthology*, 2021.

'A man on the 19.34 to Birmingham New Street...' was published online on the *Spilling Cocoa Over Martin Amis* website in 2021.

'Nets at Number 58' was published in the 'New Zealand Poetry Society International Poetry Competition' anthology for 2023.

'On the Waterfront – 9th September 2022' was previously published in 2023 in the online bilingual magazine *SETU*.

'Lost Girls' – selected for Write Out Loud competition anthology 2025. The competition was judged by Neil Astley.

'Thank Folio for Shakespeare – a crown of sonnets' was a commissioned performance piece for FOLIO, Sutton Coldfield.

'Trade and Commerce – hourly intervals of a midsummer market day' is to be included in 'Transformer – Writing the Black Country', a collection of Black Country essays and cultural literature edited by Anthony Cartwright and RM Francis.

'Backyard' was awarded 2nd place by judge, Deb Alma, in the 'Sonnet or Not Poetry Competition', 2024.

'Baiting Up' was previously published in 2023 in the online bilingual magazine *SETU*. It also appeared as an 'out of office' email poem for Jonathan Davidson at Writing West Midlands.

THANK YOU

To everybody who has ever come to one of my performances and supported me by buying books or employing me to do poetry-related things. To Simon Fletcher for editorial comments, encouragement, and opportunity over the years. To Jane Seabourne for editorial support in creating this collection. To Steve Pottinger for being in my corner. To Jean Hampton for seeing something of the writer in me and making me think I could. To Linda Nevill for being my friend, and reminding me when I need it that Jean Hampton saw something of the writer in me, and that indeed I can. To eagle-eyed Katherine Dixson. To Paul Francis for sustained email correspondence and always being up for discussing poetry-related things. Thank you also to my mum, who is sadly no longer here, and my dad for their years of love and support.

I would also like to offer a particular thank you to Keith Turley for permission to use his incredible artwork for the cover of *Unsung*.